INTRODUCTION

Python is a language that is used by professional programmers. Different programming languages are good at doing different things. Python can create 3-D graphics for special effects in movies and is often used on web servers to handle searching.

This book contains all the techniques and ideas you need to know to become a Python programming genius! Learn the basics and how to use loops and variables in Python. Discover how to create graphics, use random numbers, and build games, simulations and other programs.

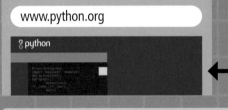

www.python.org

? python

Before you get started on your projects, you'll need to download and install Python on your computer. Find out how on page 4.

clock.py

```
def makeFace():
    b=turtle.Turtle()
    b.speed(0)
    b.hide turtle()
    b.penup

    b.dot(350)
    b.pencolor('white')
    b.dot(340)
```

The **IDLE Editor** is where you will be typing your code.

Python 3.5 Shell

```
>>>
== RESTART: hello.py ===
hello
hello
hello
>>>
```

The **Console** is where you will see any text your program outputs – as well as information about any bugs!

Python Turtle Graphics

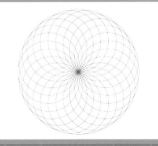

The **Turtle Graphics** window is where any graphics your program draws will be displayed.

CODE CAREFULLY AND AVOID THE BUGS!

Bugs are errors or mistakes in your code that stop your program working properly. Looking for these errors is called debugging. Make sure you enter your code really carefully. If things aren't working properly, see the tips on page 31 to help you.

⟩ GETTING STARTED

INSTALLING PYTHON

Firstly, you need to make sure your computer has the software you need to code with Python. To do this, download the latest free version from the Python website. There are some apps for tablets that run Python, but you will need to use a Mac or PC to do most of these activities. (Ask permission from the person who owns your computer before you download the software.)

STEP 1 – FIND THE PYTHON WEBSITE ▷

⇨ Open your web browser and visit **www.python.org**

www.python.org

STEP 2 – START DOWNLOADING ▷

⇨ Click the **Downloads** button near the top of the web page.

⇨ Select a version from the list at the bottom of the page. Different versions of Python may be available for your computer. This book uses Python 3.5. (Make sure you choose a version starting with Python 3, not Python 2.)

⇨ Wait for the download to complete.

Downloads

Download Python 3.5.2   Download Python 2

STEP 3 – INSTALL THE SOFTWARE ▷

⇨ Some browsers will then ask you to run the installation program. Choose **Run**.

⇨ If this doesn't happen, don't panic. The installer file should have been downloaded to your computer. Look in your **Downloads** folder for it. Double-click it to start installing Python. You should get a box giving you instructions on what to do next. Follow them to complete the installation.

STEP 4 – RUNNING PYTHON ▷

On a PC:
⇨ Click **Start** > **Programs** > **Python** > **IDLE**.
Or just click **IDLE(Python)** if it appears in the 'recently added' section.

On a Mac:
⇨ Click **Finder**.
⇨ Click **Applications**.
⇨ Double-click **Python 3**.
⇨ Click the **IDLE** icon.
⇨ Make a shortcut by dragging the **IDLE** file on to your dock at the bottom of the desktop.
⇨ Click the **IDLE** icon.

Applications
Desktop
Python 3
IDLE

I'M A PYTHON PROGRAMMER

Max Wainewright

WAYLAND
www.waylandbooks.co.uk

CONTENTS

SAYING HI!

When computer programmers start learning a new language, the first thing they usually do is learn to make a program that displays 'Hello world'. Let's look at how to do that in Python.

HELLO WORLD!

STEP 1 – RUN IDLE

IDLE stands for Integrated Development and Learning Environment. This is the program you will use to create your code. Click the shortcut to **IDLE** on your computer. (See step 4 from page 4.)

STEP 2 – START A NEW FILE

⇨ Click the **File** menu, then choose **New File**.

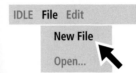

IDLE **File** Edit

New File

Open...

STEP 3 – GET CODING!

⇨ Carefully type in the code shown below:

The brackets tell Python where the item to display starts and ends.

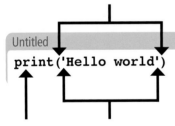

Untitled

```
print('Hello world')
```

The **print** command tells Python to display something.

The quotation marks tell Python the item to display is a **text string** (some letters).

You must type it in exactly! If you leave out a quotation mark or bracket, it will not work. **IDLE** will make parts of your code change colour to let you know you have added brackets and quotation marks correctly. Python is **case-sensitive,** which means you need to use lowercase letters for your commands.

STEP 4 – SAVE YOUR CODE

⇨ Click the **File** menu, then choose **Save**.

IDLE **File** Edit

Open...

Save...

⇨ Type **hello** as the file name.

⇨ Click **Save**.

STEP 5 – RUN YOUR CODE

⇨ Click the **Run** menu, then choose **Run Module**.

mat **Run** Optio

Python...

Run Module

```
>>>
== RESTART: hello.py ===
Hello world
>>>
```

CUSTOMISE

• Add more lines to your program.

• Can you make it tell a simple story?

• You'll need to save and run your program (steps 4 and 5) each time you add new code.

› LOOPS AND VARIABLES

If you've done some coding before, you will know that one of the most important programming concepts is the loop. If you want your code to do something over and over again, it's much quicker to use a loop instead of copying out the code several times. Let's look at how this works in Python.

STEP 1 – START A NEW FILE

⇨ Run **IDLE**. See step 4 from page 4 if you need help.

⇨ Click the **File** menu, then choose **New File**.

> IDLE **File** Edit
> **New File**
> Open...

STEP 2 – GET CODING!

⇨ Carefully type in this code. Press enter after each line.

> Untitled
> ```
> print('hello')
> print('hello')
> print('hello')
> ```

STEP 3 – SAVE YOUR CODE

⇨ Click **File** > **Save**.

⇨ Type **loops** as the file name.

⇨ Click **Save**.

> IDLE **File** Edit
> Open ..
> **Save ..**

STEP 4 – RUN YOUR CODE

⇨ Click the **Run** menu, then choose **Run Module**.

> mat **Run** Optio
> Python ..
> **Run Module**

> Python 3.5 Shell
> ```
> >>>
> == RESTART: loops.py ===
> hello
> hello
> hello
> >>>
> ```

STEP 5 – USE A LOOP

Steps 1 to 4 are a simple way to make our program say **hello** three times. But what if you wanted to make it say **hello** ten or a hundred times? There is a quicker way.

⇨ Delete your code and change it to the code shown to the right:

⇨ Check your code carefully for mistakes. **Save** and **Run** your code. What happens?

The **for** command starts the loop.

a is a variable (see page 7).

The number of times to repeat the loop.

The commands you want to repeat must be indented. Press the space key four times or use the tab key to indent the code.

```
loops.py
for a in range(10):
    print('hello')
```

A colon must be at the end of the line.

Variables are special parts of a program that store data or information.

Variables are different from ordinary numbers because they can be changed as a program runs.

Variables have a name that is used to point to a part of the computer's memory. A value is then stored in that part of the memory.

STEP 6 – KEEPING COUNT

A variable is used in Python to count how many times a **loop** has been repeated. In our program, the variable is called **a**, but it can be given any letter or word as a name. By printing that variable, we can change our program to make it count from 0 to 4.

⇨ Delete and change your code so it says:

loops.py
```
for a in range(5):
    print(a)
```

Look at how the print command has been written. If there were quotation marks around the letter **a**, Python would think it was a text string and would print the letter **a** ten times. But because there are no quotation marks, Python knows **a** is a variable.

⇨ **Save** and **Run** your code to see what happens.

Python 3.5 Shell
```
>>>
0
1
2
3
4
>>>
```

STEP 7 – COUNTING BACKWARDS

⇨ Delete and change your code again and insert the extra numbers shown inside the brackets below.

The number to start at.

Stop repeating when this number is reached.

Change the number by this amount each time.

loops.py
```
for a in range(10,0,-1):
    print(a)
```

 Save and **Run** your code.

CUSTOMISE

• Try to make your program count down from 100 all the way to zero.

• Pick a times table, such as the five times table. Adapt your code so it counts from 5, 10, 15, 20... up to 60.

KEY CONCEPT

LOOPS
In coding, when we want to repeat some code we use a loop.

VARIABLES
When we want a number to store a value that will change, we use a variable. In our loop, **a** is a variable.

› TURTLE GRAPHICS ‹

So far, everything we have produced from our code has been text. In this activity, we will look at how we can produce art, or graphics, in Python. To do this, we need to 'borrow' a set of commands called the turtle graphics library.

STEP 1 – START A NEW FILE ▶

⇨ Run **IDLE**.

⇨ Click the **File** menu, then choose **New File**.

IDLE **File** Edit
New File
Open...

STEP 2 – GET CODING! ▶

⇨ Carefully type in this code:

```
Untitled
import turtle
turtle.fd(100)
```

The command **import turtle** tells Python to borrow the turtle graphics library for our program.

turtle.fd(100) means move the turtle forward 100 steps in the current direction.

STEP 3 – SAVE YOUR CODE ▶

⇨ Click **File** > **Save**.

IDLE **File** Edit
Open ..
Save ..

⇨ Type **shapes** as the file name.

⇨ Click **Save**.

Make sure you use the name **shapes**. Never give one of your files the name **turtle** or it will confuse Python and stop it working.

STEP 4 – RUN YOUR CODE ▶

⇨ Click the **Run** menu, then choose **Run Module**.

mat **Run** Optio
Python ..
Run Module

Instead of the normal window, you should see a simple graphics window.

Python Turtle Graphics

→

The Python turtle will draw an arrow 100 steps long on the graphics window.

STEP 5 – MORE COMMANDS

⇨ Add more commands to your program.

shapes.py
```
import turtle
turtle.fd(100)
turtle.rt(90)
turtle.fd(100)
```

Python must tell the turtle to change direction before moving forward again. To do this, we use the command **turtle.rt(90)** to turn the turtle 90 degrees to the right.

⇨ **Save** and **Run** your code to test out your new commands.

Python Turtle Graphics

STEP 6 – ALL SQUARE

⇨ Add more commands to draw a square.

shapes.py
```
import turtle
turtle.fd(100)
turtle.rt(90)
turtle.fd(100)
turtle.rt(90)
turtle.fd(100)
turtle.rt(90)
turtle.fd(100)
```

⇨ **Save** and **Run** your code. You should have drawn a complete square!

Python Turtle Graphics

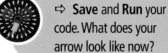

CUSTOMISE

• Try to make your square bigger.

• Which numbers need to change and which need to stay the same?

• Experiment with **turtle.lt(90)** – what does it do?

STEP 7 – CHANGE COLOUR

⇨ Delete your existing code and change it to the following (remember to use the US spelling for colour – color):

shapes.py
```
import turtle
turtle.color('red')
turtle.fd(50)
turtle.color('blue')
turtle.fd(50)
```

 ⇨ **Save** and **Run** your code. What does your arrow look like now?

Python Turtle Graphics

KEY CONCEPT

TURTLE GRAPHICS LIBRARY

The turtle graphics library is a set of commands used to move an object around the screen. As the object moves, it draws lines and patterns.

STEP 8 – TRY TO DRAW

⇨ Make your own shapes and patterns.

⇨ Can you draw your initials or even your whole name?

› PROGRAMMING POLYGONS

In the previous activity, we started to use turtle graphics to draw things. It is often easier to draw shapes by using loops (see page 6) – we can write the code to draw one side of the shape, then repeat that code to draw the other sides.

STEP I – CODE A SQUARE ▷

⇨ Run **IDLE** and start a new file.

⇨ Type in this code:

Indent these two lines so Python knows which lines to repeat.

Move the turtle forward 100 steps.

⇨ Type **polygons** as the file name.

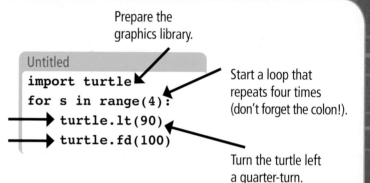

Prepare the graphics library.

```
Untitled
import turtle
for s in range(4):
    turtle.lt(90)
    turtle.fd(100)
```

Start a loop that repeats four times (don't forget the colon!).

Turn the turtle left a quarter-turn.

STEP 2 – RUN YOUR CODE ▷

⇨ Click the **Run** menu, then choose **Run Module**.

mat **Run** Optio

Python ..
Run Module

Python Turtle Graphics

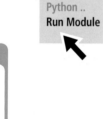

STEP 3 – MAKE AN OCTAGON ▷

⇨ Modify your code so it repeats the loop eight times and turns 45 degrees.

```
polygons.py
import turtle
for s in range(8):
    turtle.lt(45)
    turtle.fd(100)
```

Python Turtle Graphics

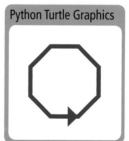

⇨ **Save** and **Run** your code. You've drawn an octagon!

CUSTOMISE

• Modify your code again to make other polygons. You will need to think about how many times the **for** loop needs to run and the angle it needs to turn:

• A square has 4 sides, so the loop runs 4 times: 360 ÷ 4 = 90, so turn 90 degrees.

• An octagon has 8 sides, so the loop runs 8 times: 360 ÷ 8 = 45, so turn 45 degrees.

• A triangle has 3 sides, so the loop runs 3 times: 360 ÷ 3 = ?

STEP 4 – ROUND IN CIRCLES

⇨ We can make a polygon that looks like a circle by increasing the number of sides. Modify your code like this:

polygons.py
```
import turtle
for s in range(36):
    turtle.lt(10)
    turtle.fd(15)
```

⇨ **Save** and **Run** your code.

Python Turtle Graphics

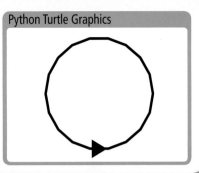

STEP 5 – POLYGON PATTERNS

⇨ Use two loops to repeat the pattern. This is called **nesting** loops. You can change the speed of the turtle by giving it a value from 1 (slow) to 10 (fast). The number 0 often does strange things in coding – in this case it makes the turtle go faster! Delete your code and add the following:

polygons.py
```
import turtle
turtle.speed(0)
for p in range(10):
    turtle.fd(15)
    for s in range(36):
        turtle.lt(10)
        turtle.fd(15)
```

Prepare the graphics library.
Make the turtle move faster.
Repeat the pattern 10 times.
  Move the turtle 15 steps
  between each circle.
Draw a circle.

⇨ Python will try to help by indenting your code. Make sure your code is displayed as in the **IDLE Editor** box here. Then **Save** and **Run** your code.

Python Turtle Graphics

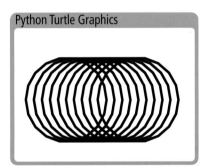

STEP 6 – TURN AGAIN

⇨ Now try turning a few degrees between each circle using the following code:

polygons.py
```
import turtle
turtle.speed(0)
for p in range(24):
    turtle.rt(15)
    for s in range(36):
        turtle.lt(10)
        turtle.rt(15)
```

Change the **for p** loop
  to run 24 times.

Change **turtle.fd(15)**
  to **turtle.rt(15)**.

 Save and **Run** your code.

Python Turtle Graphics

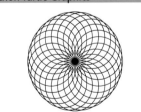

CUSTOMISE
- Make your own shapes and patterns.

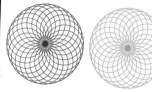

› ROLL THE DICE

When we are creating a computer game, we need to add an element of surprise to keep the player guessing what will happen. To do this, we use random numbers, which are unpredictable numbers that are made up by the computer. To use random numbers in Python, we need to work with another library.

STEP 1 – PICK A NUMBER ▷

⇨ Run **IDLE** and start a new file.

⇨ Type in the following code:

Untitled
```
import random
print(random.randint(1,10))
```

Bring in the random library.
Print a random number between 1 and 10.

⇨ Type **numbers** as the file name.

⇨ **Run** your code a few times.
Which random numbers do you get?

mat **Run** Optio

Python ..
Run Module

Python 3.5 Shell
```
>>>
8
>>>
3
>>>
9
>>>
```

STEP 2 – PLANNING ▷

Now we are going to extend our program to create a large die that is drawn on the screen and shows a different random number each time it is run. Before we begin, let's start with some planning. We need to:

1. Import the libraries we need.
2. Draw a big coloured square.
3. Pick a random number.
4. Print it on the square in a large font size.

In this activity, use the file name **numbers**. Never give one of your Python files the name **random** or it will confuse Python and stop it working properly.

STEP 2 CONTINUED ▶

So far we have used the print command to write numbers in the Python console. To make the numbers appear larger, we can use the **turtle.write()** command.

The font name, inside quotes. ↓

Two closing brackets: one for the font, one for the write command. ↓

```
turtle.write('Hi', font=('Arial', 60, 'normal'))
```

↗ The text we want the turtle to write.

↑ Type **font=** followed by a left bracket.

↑ The font size.

↑ Font style: normal, bold or italic.

STEP 3 – CODE THE DICE ▶

⇨ Delete your code from step 1 and type in the code below.

⇨ **Run** your code a few times. Which numbers do you get on your die?

numbers.py

```
import turtle                                    Bring in the turtle library.
import random                                    Bring in the random library.
turtle.speed(0)                                  Make the turtle move quickly.
turtle.color('red')                              Set the colour of the die.
turtle.begin_fill()                              Prepare Python to fill in any shapes.
for n in range(4):                               Start a loop that runs 4 times:
    turtle.forward(100)                              Move the turtle forward.
    turtle.right(90)                                 Turn the turtle right 90 degrees.
turtle.end_fill()                                Fill in the previously drawn shape (the square).
turtle.pu()                                      Stop the turtle drawing lines.
d=random.randint(1,6)                            Make a variable called d, storing a random number.
turtle.color('white')                            Set the colour of the die number.
turtle.goto(30,-80)                              Set where to draw the die number.
turtle.write(d, font=('Arial', 60, 'normal'))    Write the die number on the die.
```

CUSTOMISE

· Experiment with different numbers in the **randint** command.

· Try changing the colour of the die, the text and the font name.

· Can you add a second die to your program?

> GUESS THE NUMBER <

We can create a simple guessing game making further use of random numbers. The computer will 'think' of a random number that the player has to guess. Each time the player guesses a number, the computer will give a clue by saying if the number is too high, too low, or correct.

STEP 1 – THINK OF A NUMBER ▶

⇨ Run **IDLE** and start a new file.

⇨ Type in the following code:

```
Untitled
import random
n=random.randint(1,20)
print(n)
```

Import the random library.
Pick a random number between 1 and 20, then store it in a variable called **n**.
Display the number.

STEP 2 – SAVE AND RUN ▶

⇨ Type **guessing** as the file name.

⇨ **Run** your code a few times to test it.

```
Python 3.5 Shell
>>>
17
>>>
3
>>>
12
>>>
```

STEP 3 – ASK THE PLAYER TO GUESS ▶

Now we know the computer can think of a number, we need to ask the player to try and guess it. We will use an **input** command to do this. An input command asks the person using the program to type something in. Whatever they type in gets stored in a variable.

⇨ Modify your code by deleting the last line and adding this **input** command:

Make sure you put quotes around your text and brackets at the beginning and end.

```
Untitled
import random
n=random.randint(1,20)
g=input('Guess my number ')
```

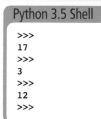

Put a space before the second quote.

⇨ **Save** and **Run** your code to test it again.

STEP 4 – RIGHT OR WRONG?

⇨ Next, we need the computer to tell us if the guess was correct or not. If the guess was wrong, then we need the player to keep guessing. If it was correct, we can congratulate the player! To do this we will use a command called **while**. This will make the program keep looping while the guess is wrong. Change your code to the following:

guessing.py

```
import random
n=random.randint(1,20)
g=0
while(g!=n):
 g=input('Guess my number ')
 g=int(g)
print('Correct!')
```

The variable **g** will store the player's guess. Set it to 0 to start with.

This code means while **g** is not equal to **n**.

The input will be a string of letters. This line converts it to a number so it can be compared to the random number.

⇨ **Save** and **Run** your code to test it again. Guess a number each time the program asks you to. When you eventually guess the right number, it will say 'Correct!'.

STEP 5 – GIVE ME A CLUE!

⇨ The game will be much better if we can give the player a clue. We can do this by checking to see if the number is too high or too low. This needs something called an IF statement. An IF statement can tell if something is true or not, then run different bits of code depending on the answer. Change your code to the following:

guessing.py

```
import random

n=random.randint(1,20)
g=0

while(g!=n):
 g=input('Guess my number ')
 g=int(g)
 if(g>n):
    print('Too big')
 if(g<n):
    print('Too small')
print('Correct!')
```

Bring in the random library.

Set the variable **n** to a random number.
Set the variable **g** to 0.

Keep looping while the guess is wrong.
Input a new guess.
Turn it into a number.
If **g** is greater than **n**:
Tell the player their guess is too big.
If **g** is less than **n**:
Tell them their guess is too small.

When **g** equals **n** (the guess equals the random number): display 'Correct!'

KEY CONCEPT

WHILE COMMAND
A while command keeps looping some code while something is true.

IF STATEMENT
An IF statement runs some code if a particular condition is true.

 Save and **Run** your code to test it again.
Have fun playing it – try it out on a friend!

>RANDOM PATTERNS

We are going to create a program that makes a random piece of art. Using a loop, we will draw multiple lines on the screen in random positions. To make the lines different colours, we will pick from a list of colours at random.

STEP I – PLAN THE PROGRAM

Python Turtle Graphics

⇨ Import the libraries we need.

⇨ Make a list of colours.

⇨ Start a loop.

⇨ Pick random **x** and **y** values for the line you have drawn to end at.

⇨ Pick a random colour from the list.

⇨ Draw a line in the chosen colour to the random end point.

STEP 2 – LEARN ABOUT LISTS

We will use a list of colours as part of the program. First, let's look at how Python handles lists. We have already used variables to store single pieces of data. A list extends this to store multiple pieces of data. A list could include things such as days of the week, people's names or the locations of objects in a game.

⇨ Run **IDLE** and start a new file.

⇨ Type in the following code:

Separate each item in the list with a comma.

The list contains text strings (words), so put quotes around each item.

Untitled
```
import random
cols=['blue','green','red','yellow']
print(random.choice(cols))
```

The list must start and end with square brackets [ ].

random.choice tells Python to return an item at random from the list inside the brackets. We call it a function.

Make sure you use all the brackets required. We need two sets at the end: one for the choice function, one for the print command.

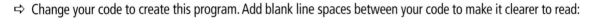

STEP 3 – SAVE AND RUN

⇨ Type **lines** as the file name.

⇨ **Run** your code a few times.

```
Python 3.5 Shell
>>>
green
>>>
yellow
>>>
blue
>>>
```

STEP 4 – THE MAIN CODE

⇨ Change your code to create this program. Add blank line spaces between your code to make it clearer to read:

lines.py

```
import turtle
import random

cols=['blue','green','red','yellow']

turtle.speed(0)

for c in range(100):
  x=random.randint(-200,200)
  y=random.randint(-200,200)
  turtle.color(random.choice(cols))
  turtle.goto(x,y)
```

Bring in the turtle library.
Bring in the random library.

Make a list of colours, called cols.

Make the turtle move quickly.

Start a loop that runs 100 times.
Make variables called **x** and **y** with random values from -200 to 200.
Set the turtle to a random colour.
Move the turtle to random co-ordinates (**x**, **y**).

CUSTOMISE

• Try increasing the number of lines that are drawn.

• Why not try adding more colours to the list?

• Experiment with the maximum and minimum random values for **x** and **y**.

• Change the thickness of the lines by using the **turtle. pensize(8)** command.

› TURTLE RACE

Python is very good at doing calculations. It can also be used to make simple games. In this activity, we will create multiple turtles and program them to move across the screen at random speeds.

STEP 1 – PLAN THE GAME

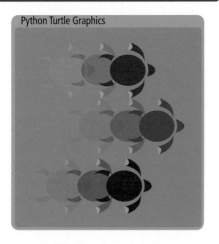

Python Turtle Graphics

➪ Import the libraries we need.

➪ Make three turtles.

➪ Set their colours.

➪ Change their shape from a triangle to a large turtle icon.

➪ Move them to the start position.

➪ Start a loop for the race.

➪ Move each turtle forward a small, random amount during each loop.

STEP 2 – MAKE THREE TURTLES

We need to make three turtles and give each one a name. To keep things simple, we will call them **a**, **b** and **c**. They will all begin from the same starting line, so we need to move each one to a different location.

➪ Run **IDLE** and start a new file. Type in the following code:

```
untitled
import turtle
import random

a = turtle.Turtle()
b = turtle.Turtle()
c = turtle.Turtle()

a.goto(-300,-100)
b.goto(-300,0)
c.goto(-300,100)
```

Import the libraries we need.

Create the three turtles called a, b and c.

Move each of them to different co-ordinates.

➪ **Save** and **Run** your code to test it so far. Call your file **race**. You should see your three turtles as arrows.

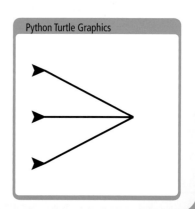

Python Turtle Graphics

⇨ Carefully change your code so it looks like the following program.
Check your code for errors by looking at the patterns between **a**, **b** and **c**.

race.py

```
import turtle
import random

a = turtle.Turtle()
a.color('red')

b = turtle.Turtle()
b.color('blue')

c = turtle.Turtle()
c.color('purple')

turtles = [a, b, c]

for item in turtles:
    item.penup()
    item.shape('turtle')
    item.shapesize(4,4)

a.goto(-300,-100)
b.goto(-300,0)
c.goto(-300,100)

for race in range(100):
    for item in turtles:
        item.fd(random.randint(0,12))
```

Import the libraries we need.

Make a turtle called **a** and colour it red.

Make a turtle called **b** and colour it blue.

Make a turtle called **c** and colour it purple.

Make a list of the turtles we are using. The turtles are not text strings, so don't use any quotes!

Loop through each of the items in the list.
Stop the turtles from drawing with **penup()**.
Make them turtle-shaped instead of triangular.
Stretch them so they are four times bigger.

Move each of them to different co-ordinates.

Make the race last 100 loops.
Loop through each of the turtles in the list.
Move each one forward a random number of steps.

Save and **Run** your code.

CUSTOMISE

• Change the colour of the turtles.

• Make them move more quickly or more slowly.

• Change the background colour of the screen.

• Add more turtles.

› KEYBOARD SKETCHER

The turtle in Python can be programmed to do different things when different keyboard keys are pressed. By making the turtle move up when someone presses the up arrow and down when they press down, we can make a simple drawing program. In this way, we are defining a procedure: creating a new super-command that combines other commands.

STEP I – PLAN THE PROGRAM

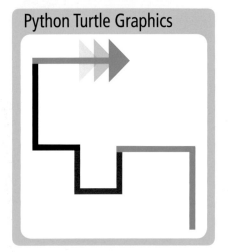

Python Turtle Graphics

⇨ Import the libraries we need.

⇨ Set the line width (or pensize).

⇨ When the **left** keyboard arrow is pressed, face left and move 20 steps.

⇨ When the **right** arrow is pressed, face right and move 20 steps.

⇨ When the **up** arrow is pressed, face the top of the screen and move up 20 steps.

⇨ When the **down** arrow is pressed, face the bottom of the screen and move down 20 steps.

⇨ When **R** is pressed, change to red. When **G** is pressed, change to green. (Other colours can be added later.)

STEP 2 – START DRAWING

We need to define a new command that will make the turtle move and draw up the screen. Programmers call this defining a procedure. Each time the **up** arrow is pressed, we will run this procedure.

⇨ Run **IDLE** and start a new file. Type in the following code:

Import the turtle library.

Define a procedure called **drawUp**. Make sure you include the brackets () and colon.

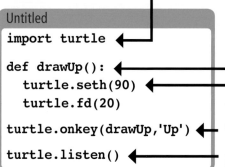

```
Untitled
import turtle

def drawUp():
    turtle.seth(90)
    turtle.fd(20)
turtle.onkey(drawUp,'Up')

turtle.listen()
```

Indent the code you want to run when the procedure is used: seth(90) makes the turtle face the top of the screen.

Tell the turtle to run the procedure whenever the **up** arrow is pressed.

Make sure the turtle is 'listening' to the keyboard and will notice keys being pressed.

STEP 3 – TEST YOUR CODE

⇨ **Save** and **Run** your code to test it so far. Call your file **sketch**.

⇨ Click the turtle graphics screen first to make sure the key presses are noticed by the turtle.

⇨ Press the **up** arrow key.

STEP 4 – THE MAIN CODE

⇨ Once you have one key working, carefully change your code to the following:

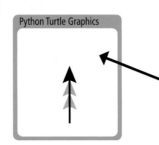

sketch.py

```python
import turtle
turtle.pensize(5)

def drawUp():
    turtle.seth(90)
    turtle.fd(20)

def drawDown():
    turtle.seth(270)
    turtle.fd(20)

def drawLeft():
    turtle.seth(180)
    turtle.fd(20)

def drawRight():
    turtle.seth(0)
    turtle.fd(20)

def setRed():
    turtle.color('Red')

def setGreen():
    turtle.color('Green')

turtle.onkey(drawUp,'Up')
turtle.onkey(drawDown,'Down')
turtle.onkey(drawLeft,'Left')
turtle.onkey(drawRight,'Right')

turtle.onkey(setRed,'r')
turtle.onkey(setGreen,'b')

turtle.listen()
```

Draw a thicker line.

Define a procedure to draw a line up the screen.

Define a procedure to draw a line down the screen.

Define a procedure to draw a line to the left.

Define a procedure to draw a line to the right.

Define a procedure to draw in red.

Define a procedure to draw in green.

Tell the turtle to run the appropriate procedure when each arrow key is pressed.

Tell the turtle to notice the keys being pressed.

CUSTOMISE
- Add other procedures to change to other colours.
- Make another procedure that changes the pen width.

 **KEY CONCEPT**

FUNCTION
A function is a type of procedure or routine that returns a value back to the main code.

 Save and **Run** your code. Now try and sketch with the arrow keys. What cool patterns can you create with your new program?

❯ THE CLOCK

This program makes a clock face with moving hour, minute and second hands. The time library is used to find out the real time, and an interval timer is used to draw the hands in the correct place every second.

STEP 1 – FIND THE TIME

⇨ Run **IDLE** and start a new file. Type in the following code:

```
Untitled
import time
t= time.localtime()
print(t)
```

Import the time library.

Find the local time and store it in the variable **t**.

Print the time.

⇨ **Save** your code, calling it **clock**.

⇨ **Run** the code and you should see the time is broken down into the year, month, day, hour, minute and so on like this:

```
Python 3.5 Shell
>>>
== RESTART: clock.py ===
time.struct_time(tm_year=2016, tm_mon=9,
tm_mday=6, tm_hour=14, tm_min=22, tm_sec=59,
tm_wday=1, tm_yday=250, tm_isdst=1)
>>>
```

STEP 2 – DIGITAL CLOCK

⇨ We don't need to know the day or year. Modify your code in the following way, so it just shows the hours, minutes and seconds. **Save** and **Run** your code.

```
clock.py
import time
t=time.localtime()
print(t.tm_hour, t.tm_min, t.tm_sec)
```

STEP 3 – SOME PLANS AND CALCULATIONS

We can use three different turtles, one for each of the hands on the clock:

The second hand will rotate 360 degrees once every 60 seconds. 360 ÷ 60 = 6, so it must rotate 6 degrees every second.

The minute hand rotates 360 degrees every 60 minutes, so we can multiply the minutes by 6 to get the angle it should be shown at.

The hour hand turns 360 degrees every 12 hours. 360 ÷ 12 = 30, so we need to multiply the number of hours by 30 to get the angle of the hour hand.

When it is 3.30 the hour hand should be between the 3 and the 4, so we also need to turn the hour hand an extra 30 degrees every 60 minutes (half a degree a minute).

We will change the colour, shape and size of each of the clock's hands:

The minute hand will be a black turtle called **m**. It will be longer than the hour hand, but slightly shorter than the second hand.

Python Turtle Graphics

The second hand will be a red turtle called **s**. It needs to be the longest hand.

The hour hand will be a blue turtle called **h**. It needs to be quite short.

STEP 4 – MAIN CODE ▶

⇨ Type in the following code:

clock.py

```
import turtle
import time

turtle.mode('logo')

h = turtle.Turtle()
h.color('blue')
h.shape('arrow')
h.shapesize(1,10)

m = turtle.Turtle()
m.color('black')
m.shape('arrow')
m.shapesize(1,14)

s = turtle.Turtle()
s.color('red')
s.shape('arrow')
s.shapesize(1,15)

def showHands():
    t=time.localtime()
    s.seth(t.tm_sec*6)
    m.seth(t.tm_min*6)
    h.seth(t.tm_hour*30 + t.tm_min*0.5)
    turtle.ontimer(showHands,1000)

showHands()
```

Import the libraries we need.

Set the turtle mode to **logo**. This makes sure it measure angles in a clockwise direction.

Create the hour hand.
Make the hand blue.
Make the hand arrow-shaped.
Make the hand 10 times longer than normal.

Create the minute hand.
Make the hand black.
Make the hand arrow-shaped.
Make the hand 14 times longer than normal.

Create the second hand.
Make the hand red.
Make the hand arrow-shaped.
Make the hand 15 times longer than normal.

Define a procedure to draw the hands.
    Store the time in the variable **t.**
    Set the angle of the second hand.
    Set the angle of the minute hand.
    Set the angle of the hour hand.
    Make the procedure run itself again in 1000 milliseconds' time (1 second later).
Run the **showHands** procedure.

Save and **Run** your code. Watch your clock display the correct time, then turn the page and find out how to display the time in a clock face.

STEP 5 – FURTHER PLANNING

We have a working clock, but to make it useful we need to give it a clock face. By using loops and drawing commands, we can add a face to our clock.

Python Turtle Graphics

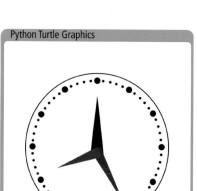

⇨ Start by drawing a large black dot in the centre of the screen.

⇨ Draw a white dot on top of the black dot to make a ring around the edge of the clock.

⇨ Draw 60 markings around the edge of the clock, one for every minute, every 5 degrees.

⇨ Draw 12 larger hour markings around the edge of the clock, every 30 degrees.

STEP 6 – MAKE SPACE

⇨ We need to make space for the code to draw the clock face. Click to start adding code before the **showHands()** command near the end of your program.

⇨ Press enter a few times to make some space.

```
turtle.ontimer(showHands,1000)
```
            Click here and press enter.
```
showHands()
```

KEY CONCEPT

TIMER
To make something happen after a delay, use the **turtle.ontimer** command.

STEP 7 – DEFINE THE FACE

⇨ Type the following code into the gap you created in step 6:

clock.py

```python
def makeFace():
    b=turtle.Turtle()
    b.speed(0)
    b.hideturtle()
    b.penup()

    b.dot(350)
    b.pencolor('white')
    b.dot(340)

    b.pencolor('black')
    for a in range(0,360,6):
        b.goto(0,0)
        b.seth(a)
        b.fd(160)
        b.dot(5)

    for a in range(0,360,30):
        b.goto(0,0)
        b.seth(a)
        b.fd(160)
        b.dot(10)
```

Define the procedure to draw the clock face.
Make a new turtle to draw the background.
Draw the clock face quickly.
Hide the turtle.
Stop the turtle from drawing a line.

Make a big black circle for the edge.
Change colour.
Create a big white circle for the clock face.

Change the colour back to black.
Start a loop to draw the minute dots.
    Move turtle **b** to the centre.
    Turn it to the angle for each minute dot.
    Move the turtle to the edge.
    Mark a small dot.

Start a loop to draw the hour dots.
    Move turtle **b** to the centre.
    Turn it to the angle for each hour dot.
    Move the turtle to the edge.
    Mark a dot.

STEP 8 – DRAW THE FACE

⇨ We have told Python how to draw the clock face by defining the procedure, but we haven't told it to actually draw it yet!

⇨ Type in **makeFace()** at the end of your program, just before the line that says **showHands()**.

     b.dot(10)

    makeFace()

 showHands()

  Now test your code and watch your clock tell the time!

CUSTOMISE

• Why not change the colour of the clock or the clock hands?

• You could experiment with dot colours and multiple dots.

• If you want to add numbers to the clock, you will need to use the **turtle.write** command:

```python
for a in range(1,13):
    b.goto(0,0)
    b.seth(a*30)
    b.fd(140)
    b.write(a)
```

<25>

> HANGMAN

In the game Hangman, the computer 'thinks' of a word. The player then has to guess the word by choosing one letter at a time. The computer needs to check to see if the letter is in the word, and to let the player know if it is.

As this is a more complex program, we need to plan it carefully. The steps to make a program work are called an algorithm.

STEP 1 – PLANNING

⇨ Pick a random word from a list: House, Apple, Pizza, Round, Green.

To make it easier to code and harder to guess, we will choose words that are all the same length: five letters.

Each item in the list will be a text string, so each will need quotes around it. Separate each one with a comma.

⇨ Keep looping until the word is guessed:

| Show the word so far. | Ask for a letter. | If the letter is in the word, show the player where. | else | Tell the player it's not in the word. |

* * * * *   **S**   *** * * S ***   **✕**

⇨ We will need to check each letter in the word to see if the suggested letter is there.

To find a specific letter in a word or text string, we can treat it a bit like a numbered list. So, if the variable called word is **HOUSE**, then **word[0]** will return the answer **H**, **word[1]** will return the answer **O**, **word[2]** will be **U** and so on.

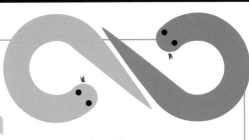

⇨ Run **IDLE** and start a new file. Type in the following code:

Untitled

```python
import random

wordList=['HOUSE','APPLE','PIZZA','ROUND','GREEN']
word=random.choice(wordList)
guess='*****'

while(guess!=word):
    print('Here is the word ',guess)
    letter=input('Guess a letter')
    hasLetter=False
    newguess=[]

    for n in range(5):
        if(letter==word[n]):
            newguess.append(letter)
            hasLetter=True
        else:
            newguess.append(guess[n])

    guess=''.join(newguess)

    if(hasLetter==True):
        print('Good guess')
    else:
        print('Not in the word')

print('The word was ',word)
```

Import the random library.

List of possible words.
Make a variable called **guess** to store the word as letters are guessed.

Loop until all letters have been guessed.
    Print the letters guessed so far.
    Ask the player for a letter.
    Start by assuming it is not in the word.
    Make a list to show any new guesses.

Start a loop for each letter in the word.
    If the guess is one of the letters:
        add it to the **newguess** list
        make a note that it has the letter.
If not in the word:
        add an asterisk * .

Join the list of letters as a string and store them in the guess variable.
    If the guess is one of the letters:
        tell the player.
    If not:
        tell the player.

If the word has been guessed correctly, leave the **while** loop and tell the player.

⇨ **Save** and **Run** your code. Call it **hangman**.

Try your game out with a friend. Remember, Python won't recognise lower-case letters when a capital letter has been used.

CUSTOMISE

• Try adding more possible words for the computer to pick. They all need to be five letters long. Make sure you use quotation marks for each one and separate them with commas.

• Change all the words for longer words – but they all need to be the same length. You will also need to change the number of times the loop runs to make sure each letter is checked.

Python Turtle Graphics

⇨ Type the following code into your program between **guess** and **while**:

```
guess='*****'
```

```
import turtle
turtle.pensize(5)
errors=0

def showStickman():
  if(errors==1):
      turtle.bk(100)
      turtle.fd(200)
  if(errors==2):
      turtle.bk(100)
      turtle.lt(90)
      turtle.fd(300)
  if(errors==3):
      turtle.rt(90)
      turtle.fd(150)
  if(errors==4):
      turtle.rt(90)
      turtle.fd(50)
  if(errors==5):
      turtle.dot(50)
  if(errors==6):
      turtle.fd(100)
      turtle.bk(75)
  if(errors==7):
      turtle.rt(45)
      turtle.fd(50)
      turtle.bk(50)
  if(errors==8):
      turtle.lt(90)
      turtle.fd(50)
      turtle.bk(50)
  if(errors==9):
      turtle.rt(45)
      turtle.fd(75)
      turtle.rt(45)
      turtle.fd(50)
      turtle.bk(50)
  if(errors==10):
      turtle.lt(90)
      turtle.fd(50)
```

```
while(guess!=word):
```

STEP 3 – MAKE SPACE

⇨ We can make the hangman game much more interesting by adding graphics.

⇨ You need to add some new code. Click to move the cursor before the **while** command in your code.

⇨ Press **enter** a few times to make some space.

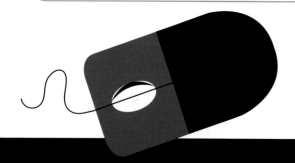

STEP 5 – LIMIT THE GUESSES

➡ Change the **while** command so it also checks to make sure no more than 10 errors have been made whilst guessing:

```
while((guess!=word)and(errors<10)):
```

STEP 6 – COUNT AND DRAW

➡ Find the command near the end of the program that says **print('Not in the word')**. Add two new lines of code below this. The first keeps count of the incorrect guesses (errors); the second runs the procedure that draws the stick man:

```
print('Not in the word')
errors=errors+1
showStickman()
```

HOW IT WORKS

Every time the player makes an incorrect guess, the **errors** variable is increased by one. When the **showStickman** procedure runs, it uses a series of IF statements to find which part of the stick man to draw. Each of the IF statements draws a different part:

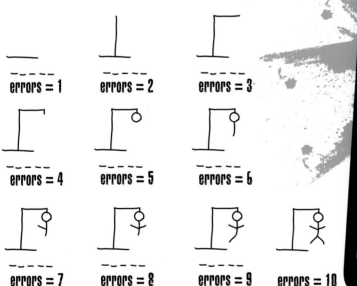

errors = 1	errors = 2	errors = 3
errors = 4	errors = 5	errors = 6
errors = 7	errors = 8	errors = 9	errors = 10

CUSTOMISE

• Modify the hangman graphics. Try making them all much bigger so they fill the screen. Add colours.

• Alter the code so that each time the player gets a letter wrong, the number of incorrect guesses is shown.

• Use the **.upper()** function to make sure all the letters that are guessed get turned into capitals. You need to add a line that says **letter=letter.upper()** after the letter is set by the input command.

> GLOSSARY

ALGORITHM Rules or steps followed to do something.

ARRAY Series of numbers or words stored as a list.

BUG An error in a program that stops it working properly.

COMMAND A special word that tells a computer to do something.

CO-ORDINATES The position of the turtle using **x** and **y** values to describe how far across and up it is from the centre.

DEBUG To remove bugs (or errors) from a program.

DEGREES The units used to measure angles.

FUNCTION A procedure that returns a value back to the main code.

LIBRARY A collection of extra commands that can be borrowed to use in a program.

LOOP An action that repeats one or more commands a number of times.

PROCEDURE Several commands that in combination do something particular.

RANDOM NUMBER A number that can't be predicted.

STEPS Small movements made by the turtle.

STRING Small movements made by the turtle.

TIMER A command that runs another function after a specified delay.

TURTLE An object that moves around the screen when given particular commands.

VARIABLE A value that can change, used to store information in a program.

UNDERSTANDING ERROR MESSAGES

When you run a program with some bugs, Python will try to help you by giving you some clues. The text that shows up in the **console** may look hard to understand, but look carefully. Python explains where and what the error is.

```
PYTHON 3.5 Shell
File 'my new program.py', line 1, in <module>
        print(a)
NameError: name 'a' is not defined
>>>
```

The bug is in line 1 of the program, right at the start.

You have tried to print the variable **a** before giving it a value.

```
PYTHON 3.5 Shell
clock.py",line 18, in showHands
        turtle.forwad(150)
AttributeError: module 'turtle' has no attribute 'forwad'
>>>
```

The error is in line 18 of the program.

turtle.forward has a missing letter!

<30>

COMMON BUGS WHEN USING PYTHON

When you find your code is not working as expected, stop and look through each command you have put in. Think about what you want it to do, and what it is really telling the computer to do. If you are entering one of the programs in this book, check you have not missed a line. Some things to watch out for:

Type commands carefully:

```
prnt(123)    ✗
```
```
print(123)   ✓
```

Spell them properly!

Check for capitals:

```
Print(123)   ✗
```
```
print(123)   ✓
```

Python is 'case-sensitive'.

Add quotes:

```
print('OK)    ✗
```
```
print('OK')   ✓
```

Use quotes at each end.

Add brackets:

```
print(123     ✗
```
```
print(123)    ✓
```

Use open and closed brackets.

Watch for colour changes

Many commands change colour when you type them correctly.

When you add a second quote to a string, the string will change colour.

Watch carefully whilst coding and the colour will help keep your code error free.

TIPS TO REDUCE BUGS

If you are making your own program, spend time drawing a diagram and planning it before you start. Try changing values if things don't work, and don't be afraid to start again – you will learn from it.

Practise debugging! Make a short program and get a friend to change one line of code while you're not looking. Can you fix it?

Indentation

```
for n in range (5):
        print('A')
        print('B')
print('C')
```

Remember to finish a **for**, **def** or **while** command with a colon (:).

Every line of code you want to include in a loop needs to be indented. If you want something to happen after the loop, make sure it is not indented.

Look for patterns

As you are typing in code, look for patterns. Try looking up and down the page, not just left to right. Is there a line of code that looks very different from the others? A bug may be lurking there.

Libraries
Remember to import the libraries you need.

```
import turtle
```
← Any program using graphics.

```
import random
```
← Any program needing random numbers or random choices.

```
import time
```
← Any program where you need to know the time.

For more information about Python visit www.python.org

INDEX

First published in Great Britain in
paperback in 2018 by Wayland

Text copyright © ICT Apps Ltd, 2017
Art and design copyright © Hodder
and Stoughton Limited, 2017

All rights reserved.

Editor: Liza Miller
Freelance editor: Hayley Fairhead
Designer: Peter Clayman
Illustrator: Maria Cox

ISBN: 978 1 5263 0064 5
10 9 8 7 6 5 4 3 2 1

Wayland
An imprint of
Hachette Children's Group
Part of Hodder & Stoughton
Carmelite House
50 Victoria Embankment
London EC4Y 0DZ

An Hachette UK Company
www.hachette.co.uk
www.hachettechildrens.co.uk

Printed in China

The website addresses (URLs)
included in this book were valid
at the time of going to press.
However, it is possible that
contents or addresses may have
changed since the publication of
this book. No responsibility for any
such changes can be accepted by
either the author or the Publisher.

E-safety
Children will need access to the
internet for most of the activities
in this book. Parents or teachers
should supervise this and discuss
staying safe online with children.